MW00938194

BROKEN
But Not Destroyed

Written by
MINISTER BILQIS IBRAHIM

xulon
PRESS

Table of Contents

Dedication

John 1:4: "In him was life; and the life was the light of men."

In the beginning, God made us a promise and He will not fail you or me. The Word that was spoken in our lives for a purpose is to be fulfilled and by His stripes we are healed.

The song "Broken" explains the core of how brokenness can take you to your knees asking God how I got here. The empty feeling like the life was sucked out of you and nothing seemed to fill the being of your soul. Something was missing and it felt like God had left the building of your spirit. The lack of knowledge of saying "yes" makes you realize how much of a price you paid for saying "yes." "Yes" to the Lord can leave you broken, bruised, and wounded. This book will express what needs to be said. A testimony of brokenness and the victory of the breath of life spoken can be used by God. After losing everything that is dear to you, there is nothing left to do but surrender to the call of God. The pain of losing all of your children or something or someone close to your heart can only lead you to a divine surrender to the will of God. Brokenness can bring you to a place of, "Lord, here I am." You find yourself on the threshing floor seeking and crying out to God for help. All you can say now is, "*Yes*." Not knowing it would cost me so much to be used by God. He has to make, mold, and shape you into His image and into His likeness.

A fresh fire and a fresh anointing have arrived and it is designed to bring about a change. There is still a light inside of you.

This book is dedicated to all those who think their lives are over because of past hurts, disappointments, and failures which have hindered us from our dreams. Today is a new day and I am here to tell you that it is not over until God says it's over.

This book is also dedicated to my children, to all my family, friends, pastors, and intercessors who have prayed me through. To all the men and women who desire to be delivered from their past and that you may walk into your destiny victoriously through Christ Jesus who is the truth and the light of your lives. It is filled with testimony and the living Word of God that flows out of my life and into the lives of others. There is always a beginning and an ending; now let our journey begin.

The peace of God be with you.

In Jesus' name, Amen.

Introduction

John 1:1: "In the beginning was the Word, and
the Word was with God, and the Word was God."

As a young girl growing up, it was not easy trying to
maintain happiness and all the secrets that couldn't be
spoken of. After looking over my life, I found there is hope
and joy at the end of a long road. I do remember some good
times and the good always outweighs the bad. As I look over
my life, I did find the enemy of my soul tried to destroy the
thing that was good in my life, but yet it took a long process
to figure out the reason for this season. This season is ripe
and for the taking and I choose to take back everything the
enemy stole from me and the promise and destiny to be fulfilled in my life. My life will be a testimony for some and a
life-changing lesson for all.

1 Corinthians 4:5: "Therefore judge nothing before the
time, until the Lord comes, which both will bring to light the
hidden things of darkness, and will make manifest the coun-
sels of the hearts: and then shall every man have praise."

I believe through the releasing of truth and testimony, this
book will encourage men and women to be free from the torment of their past. It's through the true and living Word of God
that dwells in me today is how I came to obedience to fulfill
this task and that without Jesus Christ in my life, I could not
pursue this book. So let us praise Him for the victory now.

In the Beginning

The Birth

Genesis 1:1: "In the beginning God created the heavens and the earth."

I was born in Kings County Brooklyn, New York on November 29, 1959. A beautiful and bright baby girl. Full of life not knowing what challenges I would be facing as my life's journey began. My father, a born-again Christian, converted to the Muslim faith and my mother was in the Catholic faith. I often wondered how that worked. The Bible says how two can walk if they don't agree. Help me to understand what they thought. Well anyway, as I grew up, my mother was ill. My two brothers and I were the only ones around at the time and my mother being hospitalized left my father to raise us. It seemed every time I would ask what was wrong with my mom, nobody wanted to give me a straight answer, but with determination to find out what was wrong, it took until I was much older to find out the truth. God will always answer your prayers. He is faithful in that way. We found out later in life she was diagnosed with schizophrenia. She is now on medication and she can hold healthy conversations when before she couldn't talk a word. I praise God for this miracle. My father, a young man with dreams, gifts, and talents struggled with three children and one was a girl. A beautiful girl with long hair, freckles, skinny, and meek and quiet. Didn't have much to say, but tried to understand what went wrong. At the age of four, my mother had a nervous breakdown. Moving around from house to house living with my aunt and father, I couldn't understand why my mother was so sick. Sometimes finding out the truth can be painful and it will make you take a backseat, but not knowing could be even worse. You never know what to expect. The pain of it hurts deep.

As I became older, life still didn't make sense to me. I still couldn't understand why I couldn't do a lot of things other friends and schoolmates did. I always felt like an outcast or even weird. In elementary school, kids used to pick on me because I was light skinned and had long hair. This one particular girl use to take my hair and put it in the ink bottle and I would have ink all over my white shirt. At the age of six, I began to get a little tough. Having nothing but brothers, you learn how to fight. After a while, I became the protector of the family. Every time my brothers would get into a fight, here I came to save the day. I remember this one incident where a girl scratched up my oldest brother's face and he was taught not to hit a girl, but of course I was a girl and I tried to fight her for my brother. Life after a while will teach you how to defend yourself. Guess this was my training ground for what was to come. After we moved from Brownsville, we moved to Prospect Place in Park Slope area and life started to become frightening.

My uncle used to go to work and come home drunk and beat my auntie. I couldn't understand what they used to fight about so much. My aunt was no joke; she would fight you back. I remember the fights used to get so bad, I was scared to go to the bathroom at night and pee in the bed. So my aunt would put what she called a slop bucket near the bed so I could go to the bathroom at night. I was afraid of the dark. I thought the Boogie Man would come and get me, so no matter what they tried, I would still pee in the bed. I would get a beating on top of beatings, but nothing helped. They did not hear my cry. So one night my aunt and I made JELL-O in my favorite bowl. We use to do stuff together like that and bake cookies, cakes, and pies together. She tried to help my father raise us while he worked. One night, my uncle came home drunk and I couldn't sleep that night and all of a sudden I heard a big crash and my God, my aunt was thrown down the stairs and her arm went through the glass door at the bottom of the stairs. I heard another crash and it was my favorite JELL-O bowl she used to hit my uncle in the head. The police and ambulance came and it was a mess. Auntie had stitches and so did my uncle. Those two did not agree on anything. Next thing I knew, they were divorced and we moved to Bushwick Avenue in Williamsburg in Brooklyn. I don't remember too much about it, but I do remember I met two girls who became my friend and I used to hang out at her house on Gates Avenue. I used to go there to listen to music and dance and hang out. We lived there a short time. They became my best friends and I don't know what happened; it felt like every time I got close to someone, we would move away. Remember: all I had were brothers. I searched for a friend like a sister to share my pains and concerns with.

Then we moved to Albany Avenue. Yes, they bought another house. This house was a two family house. I was twelve years old at the time. New neighborhood with a new start, it looked like we would be there for a while. My mother came to live with us and it was great. Only for a moment and then my mother started beating on me with everything she could find. I couldn't understand why she would always find some reason to beat me. I don't think she liked girls much. It felt like I was the only one that got a beating. One day, my father came home and he caught her in the act and they had a big fight. Next thing I knew, she was gone again. This time, she had to go live with her father. At that time, I had no idea my father filed separation papers. He had custody of all his children. My aunt came to live with us and I found out later that my father sold the house to my aunt so my mother would not get anything from it. I had my room by the kitchen and they always kept a close eye on me. I still couldn't understand what went wrong. After we settled in, I met some neighbors and I attended school at PS 167 for the fifth grade. I had a cool teacher; his name was Mr. Jenkins. He saw I had problems and took me under his wing. I was slow in learning and my self-esteem was shot to hell. My parents split up and I had no one to talk to. Mr. Jenkins came to the house one day to talk to my father about me so I could get some help. I had issues in life and didn't even know why. In junior high school, I tried to fit in places and with people and didn't know why. I didn't need to be popular cause popular was not my thing. Junior high was a different experience. Here I was, bused out of my neighborhood and going to a place where people didn't like me because I was black. Racism was a big issue back then and was dangerous for some of us. We were not accepted because of color. It got so bad that a group of us would meet up at the train station to make sure everyone got there safe. There was always a gang of us riding the train to go to school. We looked out for one another. This particular morning, some friends and I were going to school and we tried to wait for some of the other kids so we told some of them to go ahead of us. This was a bad decision. By the time we got to the school, we saw trails of blood from the train station to the school. We became worried. When we reached the school, we found out they were attacked by the white boys and were injured. The school kids went crazy. We set the girls' bathroom on fire in protest of what was allowed to happen to us and all we wanted was an education. After that happened things calmed down until we graduated. Then came high school and things began to get out of control. I loved music and dancing and creating and learning as much as I could. I was ambitious and still am, but walked with a lot a pain. As teenagers, we know how we try to do things and experiment thinking everything is going to be all right if we try it one time. Whether it's drinking smoking or partying, it all has its consequences. Guess what? I tried it all. I grew up with the dream I could do anything if I put my mind to it. So I wanted to help people and become a nurse. No one wanted to support me then I wanted to become a model. Nothing happened; I was told I couldn't make it there either; then I decided I wanted to dance and do music couldn't do that either. After being told I couldn't succeed at anything, I had nothing left in me to do.

So destruction started to take a stand. Rebellion set in place and I had no way out in my mind. Thinking everyone hated me and didn't want me to succeed in anything I thought would help people or in fact, help myself. After being told what I couldn't do, I started to experiment on the things I was told I couldn't. I was always told experience is the best teacher. I was told I would never be anything or accomplish anything in life and the only thing I was good for was cleaning someone's house. I remember when I used to clean my bathroom floors with a brush on my hands and knees and guess what? We had a mop. I used to scrub clothes with a washboard and we had a washing machine. Somehow I felt like a Cinderella in a modern day life. I had nobody to believe in me. As the tears fell from my eyes, I can feel the pain in my heart that had life in me and it needed to die so I can live. I began to steal in order to have nice things that my father could not afford. I looked for love in all the wrong places. At the age of sixteen, I met someone I liked and wanted to build a family with. He was much older than me; he was in college and played basketball. I liked watching the games; it was a lot of fun and it was an out so I could breathe and think about other things other than the hurt and pain. I can say one thing though: my nana and gramps were the only ones who spoke life into me. I was gramps' little princess. Yes, I was his little princess and to my nana, I was little Belle and I always felt safe around them. They always looked after us, but then something happened and I started to feel alone. I knew they loved me, but things didn't feel right. I started to feel isolated and I couldn't understand why. I loved being around people and family, but this was one of the things that has escaped me all my life. So as we were taught to dream, I would always say I would grow up and have my own family. A husband, children, and a house with a big white fence and a big yard. So much for dreams—that only lead to destruction. Every time I dream, someone destroys it with negative words. As I am writing this chapter, I still feel the pain. I need the Lord to deliver me. As I grew older, nothing made sense. I started junior high school and I thought my life would get better. Maybe a little. I started making friends and had a lot of them, but still I felt alone. I had one best friend and we were thick as thieves; she was the only one I was allowed to have sleep over. I wasn't allowed to stay at anyone's house overnight; that was not going to happen in junior high school. I thought that was the best thing that could ever happen. Then I learned about racism and how blacks and whites hated each other. The hate was so strong we needed to have police escorts to the train station before and after school to get to school and home safely. I used to go home and tell the stories and no one would believe me. They thought I didn't want to go to school. You see how the enemy will even use your family to stumble you from your destiny and pull you from a purpose. It took my Aunt Millie years later to go work out there to see what was happening. She was the only one who came to me and apologized and said, "Don't be too hard on everyone," and that I told the truth all along. That was comforting because everyone thought I didn't want to go to school, so my aunt proved that I was right. Thank you Jesus.

The Destruction

Job 26:6: "Hell is naked before him, and destruction hath no covering."

I survived that and there was some good times in my senior year when I meet a dear friend of mine whom I will not mention for protection purposes .I thought he was the cutest boy in the whole school. I had a crush on him so deep, it was sad. He never even knew how I felt. I can remember I went to every game he had. He was on the basketball team and that's where I learned the game basketball and I actually liked it. I became a sports fan. I was always encouraging from the background. That's probably what one of my overseers saw in me. That's another story. This is where I started to pull purpose out of this process of pain. Well, after the senior trip, which was an experience I learned everything I had encountered was for a purpose. We went to rocking horse ranch known as Dude Ranch and this was the first time I rode a horse. Oh man, I was terrified. I thought the horse would throw me off his back; he was wild and I was scared, so the scaredy-cat that I was, I got off and went to the pool until everyone came back from the trail ride. I was so disappointed in myself; they looked like they had fun. That was one of the good things I remember about junior high school. Ready to graduate from junior high, I wanted my hair done by a salon. That was a fight, but I got victory and that was a start of my changing over. I wanted to be beautiful for that day. My aunt introduced me to the Lord & Taylor store and that's where I got my graduation dress. I was so happy and proud that day and my father was also proud. Now came high school. I had fear because I ended up going to a school I didn't want to go to. I wanted to be a nurse and they didn't teach nursing there. I was disappointed the answer was "no, go here to Lafayette High School," what a bummer. I ended up going, but things got worse again. Running for my life, trying to stay alive till one day I ran to the train station cause we were being chased by men, dogs, and guns. I was faced with a rifle in my face and the man looked at me and then he put the gun down and said, "Just go home." Again God stepped in and saved my life. I couldn't understand. I kept asking why no one would believe me. The Word of God once again proved itself to me. His saving grace kept me alive. So as we do to get attention, I decided my life was not worth losing because people didn't believe what happened. I started skipping school and being rebellious because no one heard me, so I figured I would do something to get the attention. I started getting high off of beer and the Old English. As I look back on this, I felt unwanted. After trying the beer, I got sick and vomited, and feeling dizzy and I remember saying, "Lord, if you get me off this high, I will never do this again." The next thought was if my father found out, he would kill me. Then marijuana came into play. After trying the beer, I didn't like that at all, so I tried to smoke weed and between drinking, I thought I could kill the pain and the hurt that left me in darkness. I began to drown my feeling in drugs, alcohol, and smoking cigarettes. What a combination this became. Then having sex, not knowing anything about myself, was the biggest mistake and addiction I could have ever started. It became the enemy of my soul. I was always afraid of my father finding out what I did, trying not to bring shame to the family. Of course he got a wind of the sex part. Daddy's little girl was not a virgin anymore. He took me to a girlfriend of his named Sandra and she taught me how to protect myself. Cause once you are touched, it's another addiction to beat. My first boyfriend was a basketball star. There's something about basketball players. Anyway, he was my first, and I fell in love and wanted to get married. Then my father got a wind of that and he was furious. He forbid me to see him anymore and it broke my heart. I even ran away from home because I knew I was in love. Later on I found out he cheated on a girl in college. More pain; this was the beginning of destruction. Anyway, he was my first, and I fell in love and I was so hurt I thought all men were liars and they were incapable of loving someone. I was so hurt I became like them: hurting people before they hurt me. I had no remorse about how or what I did and with whom I did it. After my first boyfriend came many more after him. As this journey began of destruction, things had gotten worse. Trust and faith weren't an option anymore. My life became one big lie and I slept around and got high to ease the pain. Family and so-called friends didn't help the situation either.

Sometimes we bring things on ourselves, and so my life continued. Lies and deception took place. Going to clubs wearing makeup to cover up my age because at that time I was too young to hang in bars and clubs where drinking was not an option. Men, sex, and music are a bad combination. It felt like a good idea at the time, but then life became serious. Older men were attracted to me and I didn't know how to handle myself. The money flashing and showing me the best time of my life was amazing until the truth of the matter was they wanted something from me. You are right—sex became a great pastime—sex and what I could offer them was all they were after and the only thing they were interested in. This young man I met in my younger years, we grew up in the same neighborhood together where we used to go to the park and listen to the music and hang out—that's how teenagers enjoyed their time in the 'hood. He was the kind of man that loved money; he had a Cadillac and at a young age he ran illegal numbers in the neighborhood. I thought this was the thing—a man with a car—and because of my selfish needs, they supplied the money when I needed it, the clothes when I needed them, the sex to drown out my problems, along with drugs and drinking. How did I get here? I used to be so quiet and meek, only to turn into a monster. An image of what I didn't want to become. I had fallen into that trap. Another boyfriend I met was so adorable and he loved me dearly, but I didn't know how to be faithful to him and be the woman he needed me to be. He used to buy me clothes and feed me and treat me well, but for me that was not enough. I didn't know what I wanted. It seemed like every nice guy I met, my girlfriends tried to steal them from me by offering their body to them because they knew I wouldn't sleep around with anyone. At the time, I was too afraid of my father and getting pregnant, so I didn't do it. There was a time I became less afraid because I thought I missed something. Hanging out with an older crowd of girls made me feel important. I was a big girl now. When I stopped being a virgin is when my life took a turn for the worst. I didn't know who I was any-more. As time was winding down, life was a little rough for me. The men and the relationships I encountered were more than I needed. I didn't know how far this had gotten out of hand. By my eighteenth birthday, my family was tired of my destructive behavior so they asked me to leave. "Pack your bags and go figure it out." More pain. I left and went to my aunt's house thinking I would be accepted and instead we got into an argument and I left her house being hot headed. I took a train back to Brooklyn to a girl's house I met and that was a big mistake. I found out the hard way that her boyfriend was a thief. I got arrested and to God be the glory, the Lord was on my side that year. I faced a big time in jail, but God saw me through. Then I had a habit of running away from things and ran right into a pimp. Now he was a dude in a club so you see where I am going. Clubs are full of different types of characters. This is where it all began. The life of prostitution. How did I get there? I had nowhere to go after being arrested and I met this guy who introduced me to prostitution. He was not a nice person. He took me to the Waldorf Astoria and took me to a room and showed me nice looking clothes and told me to put them on and then he began to give me the drill on how this works. Then I had no idea he was snorting cocaine. What did I known about this stuff? He laid a .22 caliber gun on the bed and told me if I tried to run, he would kill me. I had to do what he said to do. At this time, it was about to get real. This man was going to shoot me. So I did what he said and I turned a trick and brought him the money and that was the beginning of my life of hell. He had no idea I planned my escape because in my mind there was no man bad enough to hurt me and get away with it. Then I met my first baby's daddy. He was cute and I thought he was my ticket out of a bad situation. Have you ever thought someone was placed right in front of you at the right time to help you? Wrong. It was just another lie and deception getting ready to take place. He was a DJ for this club and he was cute and I liked to dance. He saw what was going on with me and my pimp and that night I won a dance contest and fifty dollars for being the best dancer. I was so excited. Now that was some help because I had no money so this was like winning a thousand dollars. I felt special. So anyway, we got to talking and I told him about this guy I met and what he had me doing and how he threatened to kill me if I left him. So my boyfriend, being the gentle man he was, stepped to him and told him I was with him now and he had not better put a hand on me or they would find him in the East River. So, that made him leave me alone. Now I ended up with this new man, but not out of the business. That's what they called it back in the day. More pain. After leaving the pimp, I had nowhere to live. I was on the street for real. So this next one had access to the club after hours and we slept in the club because the owner allowed him to keep me there. That's when I went out at night to make money so we could find an apartment. So as slow as the money came in, I had to think fast cause we had nowhere to go and rest our heads. I found out I was pregnant. Now what? I couldn't believe I was in such a fix. What was I going to do? So I went on welfare and they found me an apartment and finally I had a roof over my head. Still in the business, but pregnant and afraid. Before the apartment, I slept on the hard floor of a club while I was pregnant. We moved in—my boyfriend and his friend, and myself pregnant and all. More pain. After getting stable in my new apartment and being pregnant kind of started to bring things in my life into perspective. I no longer wanted to sell my body. Being pregnant had taken its toll on me.

My mind started to think about the child more than my problems and myself. My first thought was, *How I am going to raise a child with my life like this?* I wanted my child to have a better life than this. She gave me a reason to live. I wanted to live because when you are in this life, you don't want to live; you want to die because no one will respect you or love you normally again. At least that's what they tell you. More pain. When I went to him about this and some ideas I had about opening up a business or going back to school to be a nurse, he laughed and told me how my life would never be the same again and how people will not accept me for who I am because of what I have become. People used to have this saying that you are known by the company you keep and a woman can go as far as a hole and never be looked upon as a woman, but a man can become a bum and next day put on a suit and be called "Mister" or "Sir." So my outlook on hope was almost dead, but the funny thing about a rebellious spirit is it will not believe there is no hope when you want what you want. I didn't have the wisdom to go get it on my own. The lies that keep you in bondage are so real. Men come up with some of the best stuff; you would think they rehearsed this stuff and wrote a book on how to keep women in bondage not knowing they are in bondage themselves.

The Life of a Prostitute

Hebrews 11:31: "By faith the Harlot, Rahab perished not with them that believed not, when she received the spies with peace."

B eing a prostitute was no joke. The things you encountered. The dangerous risks you take and yet and still survived. God had a plan. From running from cops to escaping death through a man who had a fantasy or his pain to cause another woman's tragedy. I have seen women dragged from cars. Literally running for their life because they may have robbed a trick or set some up to be robbed. I escaped death so many times and God still saw fit to keep me here. I reflect on the goodness of God every time the enemy brings back things that remind me of my past. Between the knives at my throat and the near deaths I encountered was only by the saving grace of God. Guns and threats from men wanting to kill me were real. Ducking and dodging bullets and knives was a lifestyle for me. The rapes were many till they became like a ritual, a way of life. It became a norm. Being robbed because you make decisions based on the money you need to bring in that night. The mistakes could cost you your life. Then you had some men who felt sorry for you and wanted to marry you to get you off the streets only to be told they do that because they want their own personal bed partner who knew how to satisfy their every need in the bedroom and not once thinking you have so much more inside of you. Still, God had a plan. Now today I find myself fighting with familiar spirits on my job at church, at school, and where I live. It never stops, so I thought, then prayer comes. How do I stay alive now that I am here? Then you become this person that has to become an actress putting on so that you meet the need of every customer. Every man's desire is different and you had to meet that requirement in order for them to pay you a decent wage. Money up front was the final rule. Then only to have a pimp that doesn't have your back could cause a problem. I was faced with going to men's apartments and risking he would cut my throat or rape me and leave me to die somewhere in a dark park. Again only the grace of God kept me. One night I was desperate to make some money. It was slow and I was tired. So this man came up in a car and said he would pay me extra to come to his house. Of course I went; I needed the money. Now I thought my man was in the car following me and to no avail, he didn't that night. So when I got to this man's apartment he pulled a knife to my throat and told me he would slice my throat if I didn't do what he did and leave me in the park across the street. I never thought I could pray so hard because all I could see is my life flashing before me. He then raped me and took me back where he picked me up and repeatedly showed up as to say, "I got away with it; I can do it again." So I told the other pimps about him and one night they jumped him and beat him bad, but that didn't kill the pain inside me. He had put fear in me I could not shake. But God. I praise and thank God for so much. As the tears run down my face I could only thank my God for saving me from a horrible death. Every man's pleasure now became my pain. I remember the places, things, and people I have encountered along the way.

The Fear

Psalm 27:3: "Though a host should encamp against me, my heart shall not fear, thought war should rise against me, in this I will be confident."

Proverbs 29:25: "The fear of man bringeth a snare: but whoso putteth his trust in the Lord shall be safe."

One morning I had a little revelation of your word for me today and I didn't realize fear played a big part in my life's journey. As I sat on my bed getting ready for work, I realized what was besetting my spirit. The Lord showed me years ago after the episode with my cousin took place I finally got an answer. Because of my past experiences with people taking things and people from me, it gave me the spirit of fear to pursue anything and made me afraid someone or something would take whatever I obtained. In relationships that are that way and it has been for years. At the job, it was the same thing: people taking and not giving back what was truly and rightfully mine. The gifts in me represent a God even I don't understand. I now know what it has done to me mentally, physically, and spiritually. All my life I experienced people taking things from me. From relationships, money, friends, ideas, dreams, etc. How my own family that said they loved me never believed anything I said and it was always the truth even if I was the one who caused it. Granted, there were times things were my fault. I don't always look for someone to blame for my problems. In the same instances people don't mind hiding behind a wall to protect themselves even if it means hurting someone else. I hold so much inside me until it scares me. I have books, testimonies, life-changing thoughts and ideas, Lord knows what else. Even as I am typing this page, I feel like there is so much more in me to share. I now know why God gives us journals. It is to put it in order for books and sermons to share with the world. My soul has been crying out a lot for answers to questions I had no idea was inside of me and yet so many things that tried to hold me back. I realize the real hold back was me. The fear of what people would think and feel if I told the truth. The hurt and pain of truth is real. Nobody likes the truth. The truth uncovers things we try to hide from others and think we are safe when we hide. Hiding behind a wall only suppresses more pain. The truth shall set you free. What a true saying. I feel like I'm being freed right now. No more being a slave to fear. The things that beset me soul are being exposed and I feel the tear in my flesh as I continue to write. Releasing the things inside are the things that will free you from fear. So a man thinks in his heart, so is he? Sins of the heart are real. We think things that should not be thought. Our desires of our flesh are a key to destruction.

The power of suggestion means to adopt a suggestion that someone has spoken into our lives. We are to guard what we allow in our spirit and we accept statements that are spoken. We need to know what is presented and its principles behind it. The power of suggestion can lead us to destruction based on what is spoken and what we accept. That it is why something as small as beautifying yourself or being smart, we worry about what people say to us or think about us. The way we dress and the way we present ourselves tends to matter to people and not to ourselves. If I wanted to look beautiful for a day, then why should it bother me what people say? It's because of the things we allow in our spirit. I hear people say to me how beautiful I am, yet they envy me when I want to look a certain way. Comments are always given. People's jealousy starts to show. The fear someone will take your beauty away from you. Fear you would be stripped of everything you are or hope to become and how the enemy will use tactics to get what he wants. Fear can sometimes make you feel people will look at you differently and fear can make you keep your mouth shut. The fear the enemy puts in your mind is that someone will get hurt or someone will be embarrassed or both. Why am I saying this is because fear is what kept me in darkness for a long time. The enemy always tries to keep your mouth quiet, even when truth affects someone else knowing the person who knows the truth is suffering inside and struggling in life to find out who they are. Is that you? What are people going to think or what people going to say how people are going to act toward you? It's all a trick of the enemy to keep you from your destiny. Women of the world do have a destiny. We do have a purpose and a destiny, a voice in this matter. Lies and deception are the worst weapons anyone can use on a person who doesn't have a clue who they are. The words, "nobody will accept you ever again, not your family, friends, men; no one will look at you the same. They will use you for what you got and throw you away and you would be back so why leave only to get your feelings hurt?" The tears of the thought that my life was over and I didn't want to live anymore, but my little girl, my little baby girl, I decided I had to live for her if no one else. I was on the corner one night at Herkimer and Fulton Street in Brooklyn and I was working that night and always thinking of how I could get out of this mess. There was this club and a lot of teenagers used to hang out there on Friday nights, partying and getting high. This one particular night, a fight broke out and shots were fired. All I could do is hide behind the tree the on the corner I was standing on. For some reason, I thought the crowd was gone, except one had a .22 in my face and he told me, "I should shoot you right here, you whore." All I could say to him, "Was would you please take me out of my misery?" He looked at me and said, "Wow sis, I can't do that to you; you are cool. Be careful," and he left. At some point my father did a drive by and saw me on the corner one night and from the conversations told to me, he was hurt. His girlfriend at the time was my stepmother and I had gotten a call one night and this woman called me and asked for me and I had no idea who this woman was. It was my stepmother and she said she wanted to meet me. I was uneasy at first, but I said what would I have to lose. So one day I arranged it so I could go back home, not knowing this was my way out of a life of hell. We met and she told me if I wanted to get out, I could come back home and I told her my aunt did not want me back in the house ever, so how would this happen? Her reply was she paid rent and nobody could tell her what to do. I thought this was the answer to all my problems—only it brought more problems along the way. God never tells you the whole story; sometimes you have to walk through the process. I thought coming back home would allow me to get my life together and move out and live a normal life. Wrong. For a while it was great, but then my baby's daddy decided he wouldn't let me go that easy. He used to come by the house threaten me and acting all crazy, like I was his property. My father ended all that by letting him know if he didn't want some real problems, he better not come around anymore. So my father had to get custody of my oldest daughter for a while until I got some backbone to defend myself. After a while, I got some muscles and defended myself. I always thought no matter what, he was still the father of my child, so it was arranged he would have visitation rights with her every weekend. I didn't know that would to start another problem. After quite a few years, my daughter's father's brother molested her. I felt like it was too late to do anything. I felt he did this on purpose to get back at me for leaving. Soon after, the brother died of an overdose of cocaine. How could he be so cruel? This was my baby girl. I love her with everything I have. It was because of her that I even wanted to get my life straight. Now here comes the process of being out of the business. I thought once I left the business, my life would get back to normal. Think again. Old boyfriends tried to date me and I didn't feel right. I started to be introduced to men who would spend their money like it was no problem. After a while, it became second nature. I still felt like I prostituted myself. After people speak things into your life, it's like it never leaves. The power of life and death are in the tongue, but with everything else that could go wrong, I still never stopped trying to get my life back on track. It was no easy road. First of all, I didn't know about God and church and how I could go and get myself together. It took a lot of soul searching because it seemed as if I still prostituted myself in a different form. Guys I grew up with asked me out and I thought it would be cool. Oh, someone familiar, but guess again. Men don't let you forget who you were, let alone who you are. The bondage I still felt was unreal. I thought to even go back into the life because I wasn't doing any better out in the world. Sometimes I felt like I was dealt a bad hand all my life. Nothing came to me easy or correct. I had to always fight my way through. If it wasn't relationships, it was my dreams or career and if not that, something else. Lord, help me to understand why I was not normal. When everybody got into things and I was there, man let me try it and I always got caught. Being back at home was a struggle. I was grown and the rules were the same. No one ever treated me like I belonged, but I endured to the end. This was a real process from the street to being a mother and a homemaker. I had no high school diploma or a GED. Who would hire me, a young woman with a criminal record and a horrible past? Adjusting being home wasn't enough. I was back in a neighborhood where I grew up and that's where he had me so that I wouldn't go back. The tactic was to embarrass me enough so they could have ammunition to keep me on the streets. This was the tormenting of my mind. To make you think you have no way out. The trick was to belittle you in front of everyone who thought they knew you and they would make fun of you so you would feel like you didn't belong in the society of everyone else. What would people think about you? Back in the day, keeping up a good appearance was important to family. You didn't want to shame family. That was an omen. Somehow, God loved me so much it didn't matter what people thought about me. I wanted to be free. I was beautiful and I knew it and I wasn't going to let a man make me feel like I did not belong in the land of the living. After a while, my old girlfriend befriended me again and I started to live life a little better than before. I use to tell my story to my stepmother and it helped the process a little. Then came the hard part: everyone started treating me like nothing ever happened. As a matter of fact, they welcomed me back to the block. Albany Avenue is where I lived for thirty-eight years of my life and there were a lot of memories there. Neighbors I grew up with made feel like I was home again. I still had problems adjusting in other areas, like dating and finding someone who would take a chance on my child and me.

Remember, I had a little girl and the question was, "Who would want to raise a pimp's child?" One thing about God is He never makes us look bad. For every negative thing this man ever said to me, God proved him wrong every time. A lot of times men didn't treat me nice, but it didn't stop me from trying to find the right one for me. So I thought as the journey continued I tried to get my GED so I could find a job. I took it once and failed. I was a little disappointed, but

I kept on trying. Then I met another young man and he was in the Navy and a friend of my brother. He was cute; I liked him. So we started dating and I used to go up to Connecticut to visit him on his leave. He was a gentleman, or so I thought. He brought me my first Valentine's Day card. It was special to me because no one ever gave me a custom made card before. So I thought this man had it all together. Still being sexually active, I got pregnant again, and that was the worst thing I could have done. When I found out I was pregnant, I thought I was in love and my life was going to be so sweet. Wrong. When he found out, his words were, "It's not mine. Who were you sleeping with?" My whole world came tumbling down. I couldn't believe he said that to me. I was devastated and thought about what my first child's father said to me: no one would marry me because I wasn't worthy. Who would marry an ex-prostitute? I lost the baby at birth. It was a beautiful baby boy.

After a couple of months, I was determined to find someone who would love me for me. Then I met Fatima's father. You would think they would let me pick my own boyfriends. You would think I didn't know how to how to pick one for myself. I guess I didn't, given my track record. So we dated for six months. I had to know this was real; I already had a daughter and I didn't want to fail at this one. I had a rule that if a man could last from six months to a year without touching me, he was the one. After getting to know him, he was sweet and kind, and after a while, I did have sex with him. We use to talk about life and our future and stuff was good. Then came the decision to move to better myself. Get out of the environment. Change my atmosphere. So I left New York for a year and the first year, I found out I was pregnant. *Oh man, trouble,* I thought. I stayed with my first sister-in-law who nobody liked. I always was a believer that you give a person a try until they mess up. So I panicked. I left New York to get myself together, not get pregnant. I didn't get pregnant up there; I got pregnant in New York before I left. They were religious people, so this was unacceptable. I was not even married. That's why he was on the base and I was at my brother's house. So I took the GED and passed it. *Now what do I do?* I had to tell him I was pregnant. He was happy this would be his first and only child. We talked about our future, but as close as it got to giving birth, he wanted to move back home. I said no. As the story goes, I went back to New York. I wanted to be with him, I loved him, and wanted to be where he was. We had talks about marriage and starting over. So I moved back after he got out of the military moved in with his mother and I felt so uncomfortable about this. His parents were married and I felt like I was shacking up under their roof. Now, I knew nothing about this stuff. I felt it was wrong and I wanted to be married if I was going to stay at his mother's house, especially with a baby. Fatima was a beautiful child. She was one of my biggest I gave birth to. So we decide to get engaged. Of course, something smelled fishy to me. He always used to say he didn't want to get married again, especially after his first failed marriage. I felt like this was a never-ending story. It felt like everyone I got involved with to the point of marriage ended up in a disaster. Now explain to me this one: he bought me an engagement ring from Major's Jewelry and it was not expensive, but I loved it. He let me pick it out. Well anyway, this didn't last long because I started to feel like I was in this by myself and he was forced to do this. The last thing I wanted was a man to be forced into marrying me. I always wanted a man to willingly do this. This was important to me. This one-way street thing doesn't work for me. I felt so rejected. How can I deal with the rejection?

This was another issue. Being rejected was an example of how the enemy would think he has his way in your mind. No one likes rejection. So now here's another mountain to climb to get back on top. So months went on and finally he decided he had to go to New Jersey to see his ex-wife. The reason was he had to get some books from her. I allowed him to go because I wanted to trust him. Guess what? Hours went by and no baby daddy. I was upset and furious as the hours went by. By the time he got home, I was drunk and pissed off. He calmed himself trying to get in my bed and I thought, *man, you have got to be kidding*. We had a big fight and I ended up calling my stepmother and she said, "Oh, you don't have to take that," and of course I went back home with daddy and the marriage was off. The thoughts of nobody would want me came into play again. I was disappointed in him; he was the last person I thought would have cheated on me. Well long story short, there was no wedding. After we broke up, he did keep his word about raising our daughter. So I wouldn't have to raise her alone. He was a great father, not only to his daughter, but to all my children. He was special in that area. So all wasn't lost; he helped me to raise all my children. To this day, my children think of him as daddy. God is still good. A lot of times, women think a man has to acknowledge the presence of your being, but that is not true. God validates who we are, not man, and we have this thing all twisted up. The only true validation comes from God Himself. I have found many will reject you because they weren't for you anyway. Waiting on the Lord is the key to anyone's success. Trust and believe I am God. Believing on God's Word is the only way out of an inconvertible situation. You would think dating would come easy after living such a traumatic life style. Well, here's a newsflash: it's not, especially if they knew you before. Sex and dating have become an addiction. One would not happen without the other. That's the way it was. If a guy took you to dinner, he expected to lay down with you that night or before the night was over. For a lot of people, this was normal. The Word of God says the marriage bed is undefiled. So why are we still sleeping around as if God never spoke? When I first started sleeping around with different men, I found out I was insecure of who I was and empty, looking for love in the wrong places. This is what got me in the situations I found myself in. Yes, sometimes we bring things on ourselves. It's not always the devil. It's our foolish way of thinking and our unholy lifestyle we live and looking for love in the wrong places like clubs, bars, and things of that nature. Once you've been touched, it feels like you have become addicted to it and you have to have it. You sleep around with familiar boyfriends because you try to change and all the time, life rapes you of your life. Raping you of your identity and self-esteem. A lot of times that rape occurred in my life came from people I knew or had an acquaintanceship with. In the world, it was boyfriends after saying no. Or after you become a member of a church and someone doesn't take "no" for an answer. I feel like I've been raped all my life. Whether I was raped in the life of this world or some man took advantage of my body, one way or another. After a while, it happened so much it became normal to accept. What they didn't realize was it brought self-low esteem and shame to be who I was as a woman. Who is man that they can take what they want and think it's okay? Somewhere, a healing has to begin.

The Baptism

Acts 22:16: "And now why tarriest thou? Arise and be baptized, and wash away thy sins, calling on the name of the Lord."

I finally went to church because I had enough of what happened to me in this life. I needed a change and I didn't know how to go about it. Until one day, my neighbor told me about church and God. She said I needed to go and get baptized. I thought my father would kill me if I went to church. This would be like a slap in his face because he was a Muslim and he didn't care for church buildings. So I snuck out to church and didn't tell anyone. I got baptized at Bibleway Temple Church and I felt different. I didn't know there was more to this than getting in the water. I actually came home feeling better. I started to have impure thoughts about my life. Suicidal thoughts. I didn't want to live anymore. But God. When you have children, they allow you to see the beauty of life. My friends laughed at me when they found out I got baptized; they thought that was a big joke. They said I thought I was now better than them and I had an attitude. I was hurt to think my friends and people I grew up with all these years had a problem with me getting saved. What a bummer. This caused me to fall back. I thought I did the wrong thing. It started out as something so simple and now turned out to be so hard. I didn't understand. For the lack of knowledge, people perish. Let me tell you, it can kill you or make you crazy. Anyway, as the story unfolds, I started to feel out of place and I thought I did this to feel better and somehow I felt I did the wrong thing. Ignorance is something else. The tormenting thoughts I started having and not understanding what I am going through can weigh on a person. I eventually left the church thinking I was fine, only to find out I wasn't. I had no clue what happened to me. I didn't want people or my friends and family to be mad at me for doing this. So I left the church. After a while, I thought I had it all back on track. Things went well for a little while, then I started to have asthma attacks. As a smoker, that didn't help either. They started to get bad. One time, my lungs collapsed and I was in the emergency room. I thank God for a security guard who saw me. Then I had peumonenia I thought I would die. My next-door neighbor Mr. West saw how sick I was and rushed me to St. John's Hospital where I was admitted. Lord, what was going on in my body? I was in the emergency room a lot for different little things like woman problems and colds and things. And one day I figured out] God can make this better; if I could get in the water again, I will feel better. So I went a second time and got baptized again. Silly me, not knowing all you had to do was one time. It was the Holy Spirit I needed and I didn't know it. I tell you this has been a trip for me. I did not ask the right questions. I found myself listening to people and not God. That was the wrong answer. People will stir you wrong every time. I had a girlfriend and her mother was the one who introduced me to witchcraft. She told me my stepmother tried to kill my father and I got scared. I couldn't understand why would a person say they love someone and then in the next breath, hate them enough to harm them. I cried; I loved my father. He was all I thought I had left who understood me. I thought I protected him. So when I realized what happened, I turned all that stuff loose and didn't bother with them because I found out it was wrong and I couldn't do what they had asked me to do. Reading and searching for truth does help clarify a lot of things in your life. My life had become one big joke. So I kept on living. I starting dating the familiar and found myself back in the same cycle again. Sleeping around for money to make ends meet. I was always told if a man asks you for something, you have to expect to get paid. So with the skills I already had, I used it to my advantage. If a man asked to take me out and he wanted me to have sex with him, then fine—he had to make it worth my while. So now I was tired of men and the whole business of letting them use my body for their pleasure; it was not fun anymore. I wanted a committed relationship. Trying not inflict my children with the pain of having too many men in their lives only caused another problem. As my children grew up, they were lead to believe I abandoned them for men in my life. I had no idea my lifestyle effected them in this manner. The pain I tried to avoid only turned into a pain I helped inflict upon them. We make decisions in life to protect our children only to hurt someone who doesn't understand why you did what you did to protect them, only to have things slip through the cracks and happen anyway. Two of my children were sexually abused as far as I know and the pain they feel I cannot begin to understand, but I do know this: no matter how protective you become, there is always an entrance where the enemy can get in and hurt my children. They will never know how that made me feel. I felt I could have done something but I didn't know how to stop it. My children were always my reason for living and as they grew up, I found they had to grow up and leave me one day. To this day, they hold a lot of bitterness toward me because of the decisions I made (some of them are rightfully so) and some they have to be accountable for themselves. I cannot be the blame for everybody's life. That's why I know God has saving grace and mercy because when I was in the world, all the arguing I did with my children, I used to go and have sex or go have a drink to hide myself and my problems, but today I face them with tears and a broken heart. Being a prostitute truly had a bad taste in my mouth after a while. When I look back on how people knew I was a prostitute, they used that to manipulate a situation. Especially family and how they use to prostitute me for money so we could eat because we gambled all of our money away. Struggling from day to day worrying on how we would pay our bills and keep the house. My father died in 1988 when my son was born and the hard times came and all I could do was wonder what happened to my life again. I had to hold everybody up and there was no option. My stepmother was in no shape to do anything but mourn and the house was headed straight to hell. Working at night at the Bank of New York was not easy; neither was coming home to four children, two stepbrothers and a stepmother in mourning for her husband. It felt like everyone now depended on me to make things better. We got by for a while then we faced eviction and foreclosure on the house. How did we get here? Everyone lost their job, even my stepmother's boyfriend, and I was the only one with an income making sure everyone had a meal. Whether it was temping on a job or selling myself for cheap to get by. Finding out I was never delivered from this horror didn't make me feel good at all. I found myself doing the exact thing I thought I was delivered from. Even in church, I still slept around and tried to find the perfect husband until one day, rape entered the picture again. Yes, even in the church I was raped. I don't think for any stretch of the imagination people would say, "How that did happen?" Well the story went like this: I worked for the city at a long-term assignment praying to be hired permanently. It was a good job. The people were kind and loved me. I became a real asset to them. I loved putting everything into my work or anything I ever did. Then one day, I decided I wanted to get into a business of my own. I knew I could do it with the right guidance. So as things progressed, I meet two paralegals named Paul and Brian who showed me the ropes. I decided I wanted to learn the business. When I finally made up my mind to sign up, little did I know this was a setup from the devil. I was asked to go over to Paul's house to sign the final contract and never once thought this would ever happen again. Still, I made bad decisions. Before all that came about, I had vowed to God to be faithful to him from this day forth and I had no idea the devil had another plan that day. I went over to his house to sign the final contract and lo and behold, this man raped me. I was in total shock and I didn't know how to react, but be in fear for my life. He was a man of God and he raped me. This was unheard of, but it happened. After I got home, I cried and ask God what was wrong with this picture. I thought I was finished with this chapter to my life, only to be reminded it was never over. I felt like I lived the same hell all over again. I ended up telling my best girlfriend at the time and she couldn't believe it either. So I decided to forgive him, but little did I know he threatened to do it again. He cursed me out and warned me that if he saw me again, he would do it again. Naturally, I ran for my life. After this happened, I thought to myself, *this is not happening.* I asked myself, *why is this happening to me?* The minute I decided to be faithful to God, the enemy used someone in church to hurt me all over again. I ended up leaving the job cause he worked at the same job I was at, only on a different floor and God removed me from the premises. I was in fear for my life. After that, I started working for HRA. Since I had a new job and location, you would think I would feel better. Well, I didn't. I was messed up and I didn't know how to get back on track. I thought God would never love me because I felt I lied to God and didn't keep my vow. I loved God so much I thought I disappointed Him once again. So the loose life began to arise again in me. The dating, sleeping around, and not making good choices. I ended up pregnant in church. I felt, *oh my God what am I going to do?* Then I decided to get an abortion—not once but three times—and you would think I had enough. After so many disappointments, then came the full backslider.

The Backslider

Proverbs 14:14: "The backslider in heart shall be filled with his own ways: and a good man shall be satisfied from himself."

What is a person supposed to do when disappointment comes and it feels like life has lied to you about everything you thought was real? As I looked at my life and was so worried about how people would look at me. It seemed as if they thought I was a troublemaker. The last rape helped me to backslide in my heart. I couldn't believe I let God down once again and there was nothing I could tell God. I was one big screw up. Making promises I couldn't keep. After my last relationship, I vowed to keep myself for the Lord and then I allowed another man to rape me and take away the one thing I felt would change my life forever. It was like I had a death wish on my life. I was a target of assassination and no one could stop it. Friends and family would never understand because they didn't have to live the horror of trying to live right and nothing but bad happens to you. Backsliding in thoughts, words, and deeds can be a problem as you begin to walk this journey. The thought of losing something that you have worked so hard for and in one moment, in one second, it could all be gone. That becomes scary. What could possibly make a person go back to the old way of doing things? Has this ever crossed your mind? Well if not, be careful; it can happen. Never think for once that it couldn't ever happen to you because it can, in a blink of an eye. In this life, I have to say if you're going to tell the truth you have to tell the whole truth, so help me God. God brought to remembrance about a situation that I left out and that was the times and life after the prostitution. Yes, there was a story behind the scenes. When I first moved back to my father's house, I found a woman name Shirley living there with her two boys. That turned into my worst hell, but was my first deliverance from bondage. At first, when I met her, it was because my father discovered me on the corner selling my body for a dollar. He took her and her boys to get something to eat and there I was, on the corner of Herkimer Street selling my body. A street corner whore. After they found me, I was asked to come to my father's house and meet her. At that time, I wanted to get out of the business and didn't know how God would do it. I was depressed and suicidal and I had no idea what would happen next. Lord, help me to write this and be honest about my feelings. After I thought about what was offered to come back home and get my life together, the only thing I knew is my aunt Isma didn't want me back in her house. After Shirley, she had no choice. So I left my daughter's father and went home. Little did I know he would come after me. It got ugly for a moment, but my father threatened him and he never tried that again. I was scared and afraid. You hear so many stories about how girls get kidnapped and beaten when they try to leave that life. I, on the other hand, was terrified but I had to take that chance. My little girl life's was at stake. I didn't want her being raised around that lifestyle that destroyed me. Making the right decision can cost you your life, but the sacrifice was worth it. After moving back to my father's house, I did a lot of crying and a lot of guilt fell upon me. I thought my friends and neighbors would look at me different, but come to find out, they welcomed me back with open arms. After a while, trying to break free of my own embrace, I tried to fit in and like I said, the power of the tongue is more powerful than you can imagine, especially when you don't know God has the almighty power to stop and do anything but fail. When you lack knowledge, you can become venerable and people will take advantage of a situation. Little did I know it would come from my own family. Yes, the ones closest to you. Frightens then as it seems its reality. My father was diagnosed with leukemia around the time I was pregnant with my son. It felt like every time I got pregnant, someone died. I remember all too well, but forgot a lot on purpose and some not realizing I did. The trip to Brooklyn made me realize how much I left out. It was either someone dying of cancer or heart attack or something; it was a never-ending story. The tears never stop; the pain feels like it never wants to go away. Flatbush Avenue is where my stepmother used to live before she moved down south. People never understood our relationship and neither did I. After my father died, not too long after, my stepmother met a gentleman from Trinidad. He was a nice person and then things started to happen. I was pregnant with Nicole and I was sick and depressed because her father wasn't there for me. He had gotten someone else pregnant at the same time as me and it wasn't pretty. I thought I would lose my baby from so much stress. Then my daughters God father came and told me how someone was trying to kill my baby and destroy me. He took me to this church and because I didn't know the difference, I went in fear of losing my daughter. When she was born at St. John's Hospital, she became sick and the doctors didn't know what was wrong with her. After a few days, they got things to calm down where I could take her home and as soon as I took her home, I had to take right back to the hospital. I already lost weight and felt tired, but I had to do what a mother does and take care of my child. After the second time in the hospital, my daughter's godfather told me to take her to this church to get her help, so I did. The pastor called me out and told me someone tried to make me crazy and destroy me. I cried so hard and she said, "Don't cry; I will help you." So she gave me something to drink and blend at home to heal my body and prayed over my daughter and me. The fight I had together with the church was horrible. Everything came against me, but I went anyway. After I had her blessed and gave all my children back to God, things went well until I started getting closer to God and then all hell broke lose. I started looking for the truth and boy, did I find out some things. So now our entire household went through it. From the fights and arguments, not getting along, and everyone lost their jobs, I was the only one who was able to maintain until things came to a halt. Then the house went into foreclosure and we tried everything to save it, but it didn't happen. The closer I got to God, the more He showed me. That's when I knew there was witchcraft involved. I fought for my life and the life of my children and family. Then my stepmother decided to go to the same church because her son was out of control. out of control. She tried to involve me in burying stuff at Kingston Park, but I said no and she took my daughter and I told my daughter not to touch any of that stuff and let her grandmother do it herself.

After it was all said and done, the house went into foreclosure. As we tried to save it, I tried everything. Even went as to sell myself short for a dollar to feed my family. It felt like prostitution never left me. I began to sleep around to make ends meet gambling, trying to get money to save my father's house. The things I regret the most and realize the pain I've been suffering as I started to mature in the Lord, I realized my own family sold me out for sex and money so we could eat or keep a roof over our head. I realize I didn't have to do it, but to bring someone to sleep with me, whether your brother-in-law or friend, hurt the most. To me, that meant they had no respect for me as a human being and looked at me as a prostitute. My family doesn't realize the pain they have caused me, but I forgive them because I love them and I don't hold them accountable. I hold myself accountable. I could have said no. I pray for forgiveness. I pray for deliverance and healing for everyone. I became afraid to even think I could become a wife, a good mother, and a successful businesswoman all in one breath after I've been told so many negative things of how nobody would want me or accept me after being in that kind of lifestyle. Men wouldn't treat me kind at all. My character and my integrity were destroyed, or so I thought, until I discovered I could still be a whole woman. Old boyfriends wanted to date me and new ones came around, but they all had a motive.

Silly me thought they wanted me and all they wanted was sex. Being on the streets teaches you some things about how a man likes to feel in and out of the bedroom. The question now became, "Who can I trust?" When men looked at me, all I thought they wanted was a good time in the bedroom, not looking inside and seeing the woman I had become. The potential lay dormant inside of me. I had dreams and ambitions, and still do; the drive in me to know I can be and do so much more is still there. I may not have the best family life, but I had a lot of impartment from my nana, gramps, aunts, and friends—even my enemies. You learn to take what you need to survive and throw the rest away. On Valentine's Day and the praise is high. After five a.m. prayer, the revelations began. I realized God had a plan for me today and I couldn't go to work, even if I wanted to. On February 12, twenty-eight years ago, my first son died in my belly and I thought I was over it, but lo and behold, I wasn't. February 14, 2010 was Valentine's Day and it felt like my whole life flashed before my eyes. All the things I thought were resolved in my heart weren't. As I was in prayer this morning, God had a sense of humor. Then I saw other things like my past and after I started to see my births and deaths of my children, my tears came. My first son, who I delivered into this world dead, came back to explain some things to me. I got such a revelation out of it and the deliverance I needed to keep my mind, the Lord reminded me how good He is. God kept me from losing my mind that year and my confidence in relationships. It felt every time I fell in love, something tragic would happen. So I looked at love as a tragedy and not something I wanted to do. Today, I realize love is not such a bad thing. God showed me so much love on several occasions. This particular incident made me understand even in that, He loved me enough to keep me close to him (Lord). Whitney Houston died the day my first son died and the testimony I received from her ministering songs from "The Preacher's Wife" touched me like never before. It reminded me of the deliverance I received and the love I received on that day. Family and friends wished me the best and made me feel loved and I was special. God is still showing me how He loves me. I'm in love with Jesus. This was a part of my life I wanted to forget—at least, I thought I would, but God. Today I feel my praise is different and I feel different than I did forty years ago. Our God is faithful and keeps His word. After all these years, God still loves on me when I need to be loved on. The enemy will help you remember the things you would like to forget. The other day I was in my living room and a memory of my past pulled up beside me and began to talk to me. I couldn't believe some of the things I forgot about. My children suffered because of people. The places we dared not go, but went. The things I dared not do, but did. The encounters I had and endured. The sufferings, but I'm still here. The reward is now great because now I can let go and let God handle all of my affairs and encounters. As this journey continues, I know in my heart the trials will come, but God is in control of everything.

The Overcomer

Revelation 2:7: "He that hath an ear, let him hear what the spirit saith unto the churches; to him that overcometh will I give to eat of the tree of life, which is in the midst of the paradise of God."

After seeing how the enemy will use your past to keep you in turmoil and confusion, I now know God is the only one who can keep you in your right mind. After all, He brought up my past so often and I tried to figure out why. If it didn't come from one place or another, the fear factor and the torment of it all couldn't and wouldn't stop what God intended for my life. The times forgotten in Brooklyn surfaced day by day. The time when I went into the crack house to get Steve was all too vivid. I remember it like it was yesterday. The daring acts of a hero trying to save a life from drugs because you know it all to well can destroy a person. After all the episodes of my life—the lies, deception, betrayals, witchcraft—I thank God for loving me enough, even when I didn't understand the madness in my life. I've learned through it all, nothing happens by accident and no matter what, God is still good.

To the conclusion of this book, after all the destruction, the lies, and the deception, the Lord has made me victorious in every area of my life where the enemy tried to kill and destroy. I give all the glory to God for His love, His protection, His grace, and His mercy. I could go on and on. The Lord has done that much for me. Broken, but not destroyed and I am still here. My prayer is for every person (male or female) who reads this book can find refuge in the journey and destiny in this lifetime. God never gave us a spirit of fear, but of love, peace, and a sound mind. Find that peace within so you may live and not die, but declare every word God spoke over your lives. So let the healing begin and let the deliverance keep us on the right path to do what is right, no matter the circumstances.

On March 13, 2012, I realized why I had to repent and forgive Shirley and Mr. Kent. It is because the two people I least expected to turn their back on me did. I felt hurt and I was angry, but God brought a man in my life that I am so glad he is in my life. I thank God for Jesus because He showed me love. He gives me a sense of being and I know I matter to him. Love is truth and His truth has matured me for the journey. I repent to God about allowing people to taint the heart of God in me. Overcoming these obstacles are an act of God's kindness and mercy toward me. Overcoming the things that beset you every day can sometimes become difficult, but with God, all things are possible. I forgive my step mother and my daughter's God father for they had no idea how they made me feel.

Overcoming obstacles are becoming more visible now more than ever. You would be surprised at how God is showing me how to get my deliverance. Last night at prayer with Elder Boyd, I felt God had a miracle with my name on it. I didn't feel well and all the Lord told me was to get to the altar and He would heal me. At first I wasn't going to go, but God spoke, and out of obedience, I had to go. God showed up and He healed me from the pain. After Pastor Boyd told us the story and testimony of the mother and her daughter being on drugs and prostitution and how her pimp killed her and because of her mother's prayer and God's promise, she was brought back from the dead and filled with the Holy Ghost and praising God. When he said that, something awakened in my spirit and I started to leap for joy and God let me know how good He is. I thought about myself and began to praise God for how He brought me out of that situation. On March 14, 2012, I said I was going to Maryland for the weekend to get away. After I decided to go, all has broken lose. I forgot my son's aunt died and he wanted to go down to Virginia. Now I'm trying to figure out what is it about Virginia that is making everyone crazy? Then I figured it out; the Lord reminded me of a vision He showed me about me living down there. I couldn't see it. Overcoming obstacles and life has its rewards as well as its downside, but through it all, I made it. I made it through the sicknesses, the pain, the hurt, and now I can forgive and live. Yes Lord, it's time to live and enjoy the fruits of my labor and love. Through all the tears, I finally see the light of day. I am the lighthouse. Through it all, I am alive. I have some scars, but I'm still alive. God still has a plan for me. The price of the cross is real. When Christ died on the cross, He died for you and me so that we may live eternally. He overcame the world and that makes us victors in Christ Jesus. Amen.

Isn't it funny when you are broken, God can take a broken situation and turn it into something beautiful? Isn't that God? His love is from everlasting to everlasting.

Biography

O n November 29, 1959, I was born in Kings County, Brooklyn, New York. I am the second child and only girl of four children. I obtained my GED from the State of Connecticut Board of Education. I continued my studies in pursuit of my Bachelor's Degree at Nyack College. I have several certificates in Clerical Studies and Evangelism. I received Accredited Certifications in both the Old Testament and New Testament studies.

I participated and served on many auxiliaries, such as the feeding of 5000, outreach programs, women's ministry, intercessory prayer groups, usher boards, several speaking engagements, chaplain over the singles ministry, and also prison ministry. I am currently president over the women's ministry at The Greater Springfield Community Church in Queens.

This book was written to reach the brokenhearted to let them know they are not alone. This is a little of my life's experiences and journey of pain and recovery, and triumph and victory. This book is not only for women; it is also an empowerment for men as well. Everyone has had a broken period in their life when they felt like giving up, but God brought them back. As the story is told, Jesus reaches out His hand to lift you up. I experienced His hand and picking me up. If He can do it for me, He surely can do it for you.

My prayer is with the trust, hope, and faith, you know there is a God who loves you. The journey of *Broken, but Not Destroyed* and the trials and triumphs of a woman and man of God know what victory feels like. He carried me through it all. I am *Broken, but Not Destroyed.*

CPSIA information can be obtained
at www.ICGtesting.com
Printed in the USA
BVHW071622080820
585883BV00007B/157

9 781498 483759